At Home with Science

Munch! Crunch!

What's for lunch?

Written by Janice Lobb
Illustrated by Peter Utton and Ann Savage

KINGFISHER

NEW YORK

KINGFISHER
Larousse Kingfisher Chambers Inc.
95 Madison Avenue
New York, New York 10016

First published in 2000
10 9 8 7 6 5 4 3 2 1

ITR/0400/SC/FR/128MAWA

Created and designed by Snapdragon Publishing Ltd

LIBRARY OF CONGRESS CATALOGING-IN-PUBLICATION DATA
has been applied for.

ISBN 0-7534-5246-4

Printed in Hong Kong

Author Janice Lobb
Illustrators Peter Utton and Ann Savage

For Snapdragon
Editorial Director Jackie Fortey
Art Director Chris Legee
Designers Chris Legee and Rob Green

For Kingfisher
Series Editor Emma Wild
Series Art Editor Mike Buckley
DTP Coordinator Nicky Studdart
Production Caroline Jackson

Contents

About this book

Making popcorn in the kitchen doesn't seem like science, does it? But it is, and so is watching a loaf of bread rise or making Jell-O wobble. This book is about the science that is happening every day in your kitchen. Look around you, and you'll make some surprising discoveries.

Hall of Fame

Archie and his friends are here to help you. They are each named after famous scientists—apart from Bob the (rubber) Duck, who is just a young scientist like you!

Archie

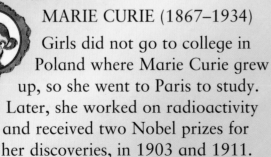

ARCHIMEDES (287–212 B.C.)
The Greek scientist Archimedes figured out why things float or sink while he was in the bathtub. According to the story, he was so pleased that he leaped up, shouting "Eureka!" which means "I've done it!"

Frank

BENJAMIN FRANKLIN (1706–1790)
Besides being one of the most important figures in American history, he was also a noted scientist. In a dangerous experiment in which he flew a kite in a storm, he proved that lightning is actually electricity.

Marie

MARIE CURIE (1867–1934)
Girls did not go to college in Poland where Marie Curie grew up, so she went to Paris to study. Later, she worked on radioactivity and received two Nobel prizes for her discoveries, in 1903 and 1911.

Dot

DOROTHY HODGKIN (1910–1994)
Dorothy Hodgkin was a British scientist, who made many important discoveries about molecules and atoms, the tiny particles that make up everything around us. She was given the Nobel prize for Chemistry in 1964.

See for yourself!

1 Read about the science in your kitchen, then try the "See for yourself!" experiments to discover how it works. In science, experiments try to find or show the answers.

2

Carefully read the instructions for each experiment, making sure you follow the numbered instructions in the correct order.

3 Here are some of the things you will need. Have everything ready before you start each experiment.

Deep pan

Frying pan

Bean sprout seeds

Glass jars

Measuring cup

Mixing bowl and spoon

Sock

Tennis ball

Old tableware

Notebook and pencil

Popcorn

Iron nails

4 Safety first! ✋

Some scientists take risks to make their discoveries, but our experiments are safe. Just make sure that you tell an adult what you are doing, and get their help when you see the red warning sign.

Amazing facts

You'll notice that some words are written in *italics*. You can learn more about them in the glossary at the back of the book. And if you want to find out some amazing facts, keep an eye out for the "Wow!" features.

WOW!

Keep an eye out for useful tips!

Have fun!

Why do I need food?

Food is tasty to eat, but we also need it to stay alive. It gives us the *energy* to move and it keeps our bodies working. Food also helps make our bodies grow and stay healthy. From birth, tiny building blocks called *cells,* which make up our bodies, have to be repaired and replaced. The *nutrients* needed for the growth and repair of cells comes from the food we eat.

> I need to balance my diet!

> What did the scale say to the bag of sugar?

Energy for life

Green plants use energy from sunlight to make their food.

Sunlight

Lettuce

Potato

Lettuce for salads

Potatoes for french fries

We can't produce our own food, so we eat and *digest* food made from plants or animals for the energy to grow and stay healthy.

A balanced diet

To stay healthy, we need to eat a mixture of foods, which give us the nutrients our bodies need.

We need *proteins* from foods, like meat, poultry, and fish, to build and repair the cells in our bodies.

Eggs

Fish

Dried beans

Meat

Potato

Bread

Rice

Pasta

Our bodies need energy from starchy and sugary foods, called *carbohydrates*, to do things like running and staying warm.

Some *fats* provide energy, and can be stored in the body for later use.

Butter

Olive Oil

Vitamins and *minerals* from other foods keep our bodies working properly.

Fruit

Vegetables

Cheese

Brown bread

See for yourself!

1 Try this simple test for fat. Press a piece of food, such as a french fry or a piece of cheese, against a thin sheet of paper.

2 Hold the paper up to the light. If the food contains a lot of fat, you will see a greasy stain.

Stain

WOW! Limeys!

In the past, sailors on long sea voyages couldn't always get enough fresh vegetables and fruit. Many became sick with scurvy, a disease caused by a lack of vitamins. Drinking lime juice, which is rich in vitamin C, helped to prevent this. This is why British sailors were given the nickname "Limeys."

Make sure you eat a balanced diet.

What makes me feel hungry?

How do you feel when you are hungry? If your body is not getting the nutrients it needs to give it energy, you may feel tired, or have a headache. This is because your brain needs a sugar, called *glucose*, which gives it energy. Glucose is carried in your blood from your stomach to your brain. When the supply runs low, the brain's energy gauge tells you that you feel hungry. If you eat or drink something to give you glucose, you stop feeling hungry.

Why do tummies rumble when they're hungry?

Because they can't talk!

Filling up

Empty Full

Hungry!

Sugary foods give you a quick energy boost, but you can feel hungry again soon after you have eaten.

Cake

Chocolates

Candy bar   Cookies

Pure glucose goes straight from your stomach into your bloodstream.

Foods containing starch give a slow, steady supply of glucose. This is better because you don't feel hungry again so quickly.

Starchy foods are digested in long, winding tubes called the *intestines*.

Potato

Bread

Rice

Pasta

Sweet potatoes

Empty Full

Full!

Intestines

Starchy foods also leave you feeling nice and full. Nerves in the wall of your stomach send "full" messages to your brain.

See for yourself!

1 Try keeping a diary of what you have eaten for two or three days. Make a note of every time you feel hungry, then think about how long it has been since you last had something to eat or drink.

Apple

Granary bar

Grapes

Ice cream

2 Look carefully at what you eat and drink. Does it contain glucose or starch? How soon do you feel full? How long before you feel hungry again?

Banana

Milk

Cheese sandwich

3 Look at your results. You should find that a square meal containing a balance of carbohydrates, proteins, and vitamins keeps you going. Fatty foods also give your body energy, but they are not good for keeping your brain alert.

Rice

Potato

Rice and potatoes are common carbohydrates.

Rumbling tummy

WOW!

If your tummy is empty, you feel hungry. Your brain knows when your body is ready for its next meal, so it makes the tummy muscles tighten. This shakes up the liquid in your tummy, and makes a rumbling sound.

Eating more than you need can make you gain weight!

Why do I get thirsty?

Water is one of the most important substances in our bodies. We cannot live without it. We can survive longer without food than without water. Nearly two thirds of our body is water. We lose a small amount each time we go to the bathroom, breathe, sweat, or cry. Water is necessary to keep our blood flowing. When the blood becomes too *concentrated*, or thick, we feel thirsty.

What would you call five bottles of soda?

A pop group!

See for yourself!

1 Bean sprout seeds show you how important water is. Take some seeds and place them on top of a piece of damp paper towel on a tray. Leave them for a few days and keep them damp and warm.

2 Then take a look. At first the beans looked lifeless. But when they took in water from the paper towel, they swelled up. After a few days, the beans sprouted and shoots appeared. The water made it possible for them to begin to grow.

The seeds cannot grow because they contain very little water.

Dried beans

Damp paper towel

The seeds soak up water and begin to sprout.

Little shoots

Keeping a balance!

You replace the water you lose by drinking and eating. Food, especially fruit and vegetables, contains a surprising amount of water.

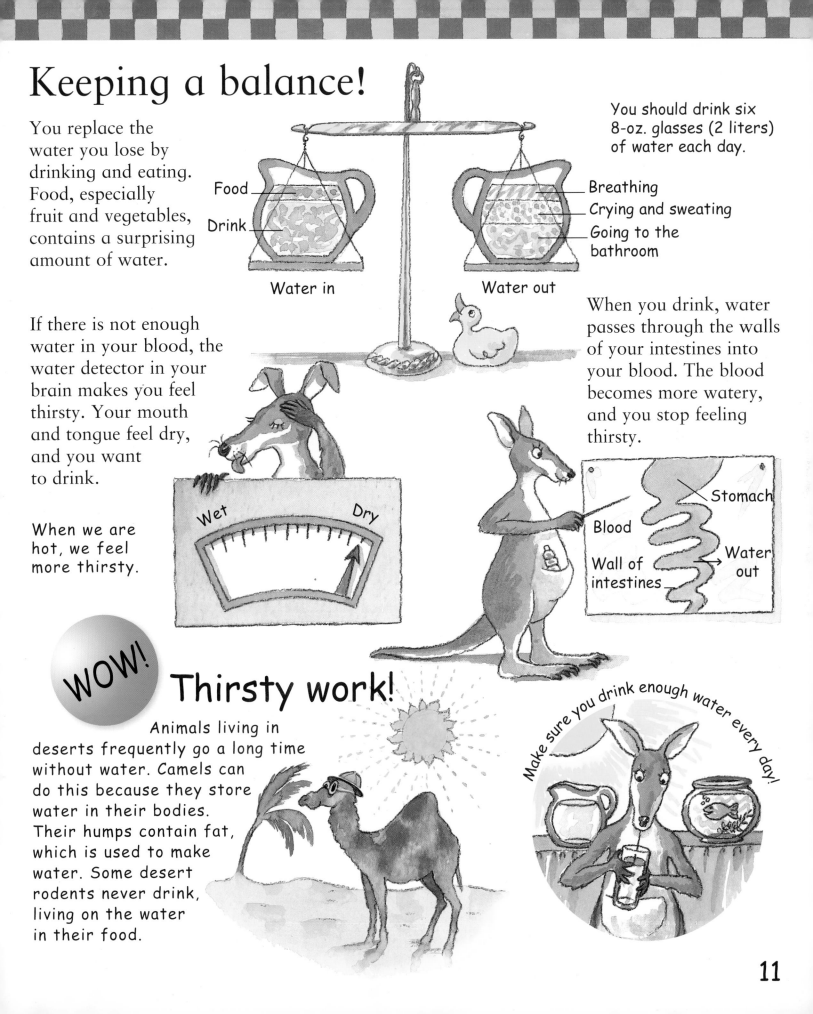

Food
Drink

Water in

Breathing
Crying and sweating
Going to the bathroom

Water out

You should drink six 8-oz. glasses (2 liters) of water each day.

If there is not enough water in your blood, the water detector in your brain makes you feel thirsty. Your mouth and tongue feel dry, and you want to drink.

When we are hot, we feel more thirsty.

Wet   Dry

When you drink, water passes through the walls of your intestines into your blood. The blood becomes more watery, and you stop feeling thirsty.

Stomach
Blood
Wall of intestines
Water out

WOW!

Thirsty work!

Animals living in deserts frequently go a long time without water. Camels can do this because they store water in their bodies. Their humps contain fat, which is used to make water. Some desert rodents never drink, living on the water in their food.

Make sure you drink enough water every day!

Why is food tasty?

Our *senses* tell us about the food we eat. We like it to taste and smell good. Your tongue is covered with tiny bumps. On the sides of these are *taste buds*. They tell you what food tastes like as you chew it. Each bud can only sense one of four flavors—salty, sweet, sour, and bitter. Your tongue, however, tastes a mixture of these flavors when you eat. And the scents that your nose smells help you enjoy food even more.

What has buds but never flowers?

Your tongue!

Tastes and smells

Patches of taste buds on different parts of your tongue taste different flavors. As you chew, food mixed with saliva passes over them, and they send a taste message to your brain.

Sweet
Sour
Bitter
Salty

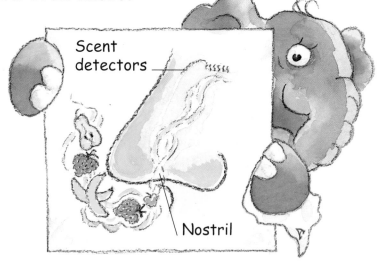

Scent detectors

Nostril

Inside your nose, at the top, are special detectors that pick up scents. When you have a cold, food isn't very tasty because you cannot taste it or smell it properly.

12

See for yourself!

 1 Try testing your own taste buds. Start by labeling three cups—"salty," "sour," and "sweet."

Sour

2 Fill the cups half way with water. Stir half a teaspoon of table salt into the "salty" cup, lemon juice into the "sour" one, and sugar into the "sweet" cup.

Salty   Sour   Sweet

Salt   Lemon juice   Sugar

3 Place a tiny drop of one flavor on different parts of your tongue (the tip and the edges work best). Try the lemon juice first. Then test the other flavors one by one.

Which part of your tongue tastes the sour lemon juice?

Fiery flavors

WOW!

Have you ever eaten food that contains chili peppers, like hot Mexican salsa? Hot foods, like chili peppers and mustard oil, make your mouth feel as if it is burning, but hot is not a flavor that your taste buds can sense. You feel it with the sides of your mouth as well as your tongue. They are telling your brain "Ow! That hurts."

Not everything that looks good tastes good!

13

Why does food go bad?

If food turns squashy or smelly, we say that it has gone bad or is rotten. It has been changed by tiny living things called *bacteria* and *mold* that feed and grow on food by breaking it down with chemicals called *enzymes*. Food goes bad more quickly when kept in warm places because bacteria and mold grow faster there, so we keep food cool in the refrigerator.

A moldy elephant!

What's big and green and has a trunk?

See for yourself!

1 Put some pieces of ripe fruit or vegetables into a jam jar or a small plastic pot and cover them. Leave the container in a warm place for a few days.

2 Look carefully at the food through a magnifying glass. What do you see?

Fresh fruit

Moldy fruit

Mold

A clean kitchen!

Some bacteria in food make poisons that can make us sick. This is why it is important to keep everything in the kitchen clean.

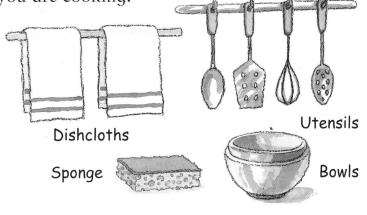

Always wash raw fruit and vegetables before you eat them.

Always use clean equipment when you are cooking.

Dishcloths

Sponge

Utensils

Bowls

Do not let raw, uncooked meat touch cooked meat. Bacteria found on the raw meat can be picked up by the cooked meat.

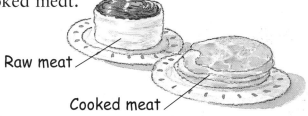

Raw meat

Cooked meat

Make sure you store cooked and uncooked food separately.

Store raw meat on the bottom shelf of the fridge.

Moldy medicine!

WOW!

Mold

Medicine

An important medicine called penicillin is made from the green mold that grows on fruit. Penicillin is a type of medicine called an antibiotic, which helps us to fight germs.

Mold

Remember to wash your hands before eating!

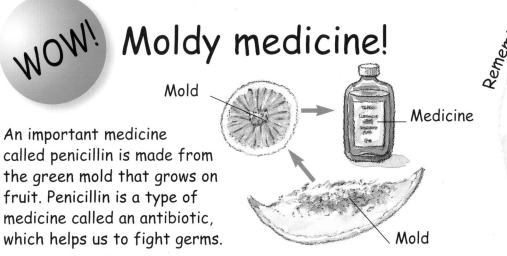

How is food kept fresh?

Long ago, people would go hungry when they ran out of fresh food. Today, we have ways of keeping food fresh for a long time and we can eat what we want throughout the year. In order to do this, the bacteria, molds, and enzymes that make food go bad have to be destroyed or slowed down. There are several ways of doing this: food can be made very dry, kept cold, or mixed with special chemicals called *preservatives*.

Why did the baby strawberry cry?

Because his parents were in a jam!

Stop the rot!

Food will keep fresh for months in a freezer and for days in a fridge, but as soon as the food warms up again, it will start to go bad.

Fresh peas   Frozen peas

If the food is frozen, bacteria can't grow.

Water can be taken out of food by drying it in the sun, in kilns, or in smoke houses. Food can also be freeze-dried.

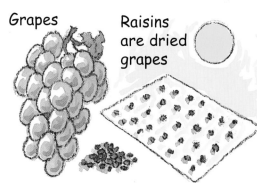

Grapes

Raisins are dried grapes

Bacteria and mold cannot live in dry food.

Sugar, salt, vinegar, and other chemicals are used to preserve food.

Heating food and storing it in sealed jars or cans will make it last for many years.

Heat kills off any bacteria in the food.

See for yourself! ✋

1 Try some different ways of preserving food. Peel two potatoes carefully and then cut them into six strips. Ask an adult to help you with this.

2 Place the strips on three small dishes, and cover one strip with salt, one with sugar, and leave one as it is.

Sugar

Plain

Salt

3 Put one strip on a piece of paper in a warm, dry place. Wrap two separately in plastic wrap, and put one in the fridge and one in the freezer.

Plastic wrap

4 After a week, examine the strips and see which ones are still fresh. Try using the same methods with other vegetables or fruit, and compare the results.

Ice houses

WOW!

Before fridges were invented, people used ice to keep food fresh. An ice house was usually covered by a mound of earth to keep it cool. The ice was brought there in blocks, which would not melt for up to a year if they were packed tightly in straw.

Check the "best before" date on foods in your cupboards and fridge.

Why does bread rise?

If you look closely at a slice of bread, you can see that it is full of little holes. These holes make it light and fluffy. Bread is made by adding a tiny *fungus* called yeast to the flour and other ingredients. When the bread is left to rise, the yeast converts the sugar in the dough mixture into alcohol and a gas called *carbon dioxide*. The holes we see are full of this gas and they make the dough expand. When the bread is baking the alcohol evaporates in the heat of the oven.

What did the oven say to the dough?

Don't loaf around!

A bubbly mixture

Raw dough rises because the yeast is making lots of gas bubbles. If you have some fast-action yeast in your store cupboard try mixing it with warm water and some sugar.

Yeast

Sugar

Warm water

Risen dough

Little bubbles of carbon dioxide form in the dough as the bread rises.

Baked bread

Bubbles

As the dough rises, the gas bubbles start to expand and get even bigger. When the dough is cooked, it sets around the bubbles so that they do not collapse or escape.

See for yourself!

1 Try making your own bread rolls. If you have a packet of yeast, you should find a recipe on the back, or you can use bread mix if you prefer. Follow the instructions carefully.

Bread mix

2 When you have mixed all the ingredients together, cut through the dough carefully and take a look.

Little bubbles forming

3 After you have left the dough to rise, feel the difference. Press it with your finger and see what happens. Then try cutting through the dough again.

4 Finally, cook your rolls. When they are cool, they should be light and firm to the touch. All the changes in the dough are permanent.

What a gas!

The bubbles of gas in fizzy drinks are just the same as those in bread and cakes—carbon dioxide—but they can escape! They can make your nose feel quite tickly while you are drinking.

WOW!

Don't overcook your rolls or they will burn and turn black!

What happens after I swallow?

Do you ever wonder what happens to your food after you have swallowed it? Like all animals, we need to digest our food. It is one of the things that makes us different from most plants. The food we eat needs to be broken down into simpler, smaller substances that can nourish our bodies. This happens in the part of your body called the *alimentary canal*, which starts at the mouth and ends at the anus. As the food moves from one end of the body to the other, it is broken down and squeezed through the canal by strong muscles along the canal wall.

What goes "Quick, quick"?

A duck with hiccups!

See for yourself!

1 To see how food travels through your alimentary canal, find a sock and a tennis ball. Put the ball into the open end of the sock.

2 Then close the end of the sock with one hand, and use the other to squeeze the ball toward the toe of the sock.

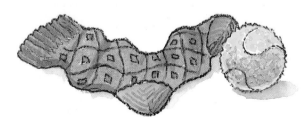

This shows how food is pushed along the canal by muscles in the canal wall.

Follow your food

You use your teeth to chew food into tiny pieces. After swallowing, it passes through a tube called the esophagus into your stomach.

The stomach is like a stretchy bag that expands to hold food. Thick muscles in its wall churn the food with *acid* and enzymes, substances that break down the food even more.

Then it moves into a long, thin tube called the small intestine, where the food is digested by more enzymes. Finally, the food's nutrients pass through the intestine wall and into the bloodstream, which goes to all parts of your body.

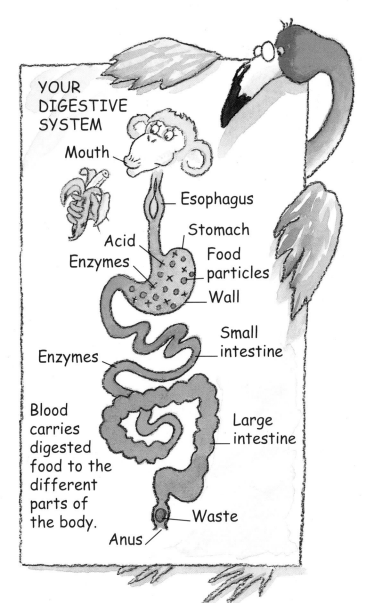

YOUR DIGESTIVE SYSTEM

Mouth

Esophagus

Acid
Enzymes

Stomach
Food particles
Wall

Enzymes

Small intestine

Blood carries digested food to the different parts of the body.

Large intestine

Waste

Anus

WOW! Stomach stones

Some animals and birds swallow stones to help them grind the food in their stomachs. Some stones, called gastroliths, have even been discovered alongside dinosaur fossils. They were worn smooth after years of tumbling around inside the dinosaur's stomach, grinding up tough leaves and twigs.

You go to the bathroom to get rid of water and food your body doesn't need.

Why does Jell-O wobble?

Have you ever carried some wobbly Jell-O? It wobbles because it is mostly made of water. Jell-O is held together by gelatin, a *gelling agent* used in cooking to set liquids. Gelatin is an animal protein. Agar, another gelling agent, is a jellylike substance that comes from seaweed. Because they have no color or taste, they can be added to main course or dessert dishes. They are also clear, so if you put pieces of fruit in Jell-O, you can see them.

What wobbles and can fly?

A Jell-Ocopter!

How gelatin sets

When gelatin powder is mixed with boiling water, it dissolves to make a *colloid*.

While it is still hot, the Jell-O is runny and can be poured into a mold.

When the Jell-O cools, it sets and becomes a solid called a gel. A gel can be made up of almost all water, but the water is trapped and does not run.

See for yourself! ✋

1 Try making some Jell-O. Ask an adult to help you with this. Find three small molds. Follow the instructions on the Jell-O box, dissolving the powder in boiling water.

2 Let the Jell-O cool a little, then pour it into the molds. Fill up the molds with cold water and stir. Put a different amount of water in each mold.

3 Leave the Jell-O to set. Then take a look. If you have used less water than the recipe says, the Jell-O will be stiffer and hold its shape well. If you have used more water, the Jell-O will be very wobbly.

Right amount of water   Less water   More water

4 Now try making some fizzy Jell-O. When the Jell-O is dissolved, let it cool and add some soda water or lemon-lime soft drink. The bubbles will be trapped as the Jell-O sets.

 WOW!

Collywobbles!

Colloids are not just found in food, they are everywhere. They are in everything that is slimy, sticky, or wobbly, such as glue and hair gel. All living things are made partly of colloids, from bacteria and rubber trees to slugs and sharks—and even you!

Fruit contains pectin, a gelling agent that helps set jam.

Why does butter melt?

What did the dish say to the butter?

Don't slip away!

Cold butter taken out of the fridge is hard. But if you put it in a warm place, it becomes soft enough to spread on bread, and if you heat it in a pan, it becomes runny. Butter melts because it turns easily from a solid into a liquid. A solid is something that stays the same shape and size. A liquid is something that changes its shape to fit its container. Solid butter can stand on a plate, but melted butter needs a container to stop it from spilling everywhere.

See for yourself!

1 Put a slice of butter, a piece of chocolate, a piece of wax candle, and a sugar cube on a plastic plate, and place it on a sunny windowsill.

Wax

Chocolate

Butter

Sugar

Warmth from the sun

2 Leave the plate for an hour, and then look at each one in turn. What changes can you see? Which of them has begun to melt?

What differences do you see?

The melting point!

When some solids are heated, you can see them change from solid into liquid. This change takes place at their *melting point*. You can see this when you watch the wax melting on a candle (only do this with an adult).

It doesn't take much heat to melt butter because it has a low melting point. So do many plastics, which is why plastic bowls are not used on the stove or in the oven.

Plastic bowl

Plastic melts

Never put anything plastic on a hot stove.

The materials used to make pots and pans for cooking, like metal or glass, will heat up without melting because they have a high melting point.

Never touch hot pans.

Metal pan

All churned up!

WOW!

Do you know that 2 gallons of milk only produces a pound of butter? Butter is made from milk fat, which is separated from cream by shaking or churning it. In the past, churns were made of wood or stone and operated by hand. It could take over an hour for the butter to form. It only takes a few seconds with modern machinery.

Wooden butter churn

Don't put chocolate in your pocket—it might melt!

25

Why does corn pop?

Have you ever wondered how a small, hard *kernel* of corn can turn into a fluffy piece of popcorn? When a corn kernel is heated in some oil, it gets hot quickly. Inside the kernel, there is a tiny amount of water that turns into steam and causes a small explosion.

The kernel's tough skin splits as the *starch* inside expands to several times its usual size, and a lot of air gets into it. Starch is the corn's energy store and when we eat it, it gives us energy, too.

What did the popcorn say to the rice crispies?

I'm puffed out!

Exploding seeds

Plants in the grass family, like corn, wheat, and rice, store starch in their *grains*. The grains use this saved energy to sprout and grow into new plants.

When they are hard, grains can be difficult to digest, but we can eat them if they are made light and fluffy.

Wheat

These three plants are called cereal plants.

Corn

Rice

Potatoes store starch in stems under the ground.

Potato

See for yourself! ✋

1 Try popping your own corn. You can buy popcorn to make on the stove or special packs for the microwave.

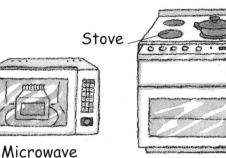

Stove

Microwave

2 Cooking popcorn on the stove makes it easier to see what is going on, but you need an adult to help you. You will need some oil and a deep pan with a lid.

Oil

Kernels

3 Follow the instructions on the pack. After the corn has been put in the heated oil, listen carefully. What can you hear?

Pop!   Pop!

4 When the popcorn is ready, pour it into a bowl. Compare the cooked corn with the uncooked kernels. What are the differences? Then add a little butter and salt, and enjoy eating it!

Cooked

Uncooked

WOW! Stiff and starchy!

Starchy powder made from cereal plants and potatoes has many uses. It is used to make paper and glue, and it is also made into flour for thickening food. Starch used to stiffen clothes before ironing is made from white rice. People who are rather stiff and precise are sometimes described as "starchy."

Keep an eye out for puffed grains at breakfast, too!

27

Why are pans made of metal?

Most of the pans we use for cooking are made of metals. This is because they are good *conductors* of heat. Metal pans get hot because heat moves through them quickly, which is important if food is to be cooked evenly. Metals are used in pans because they have very high melting points, so they never get hot enough to melt while on the stove. Cooking pots and pans are usually made of iron, copper, or aluminum, which are often mixed with other metals to make them strong and durable.

What did the saucepan say to the orchestra?

I'm a good conductor!

Conducting heat

Before it is heated, a metal pan feels cold to the touch because it draws heat away from your skin.

When the base of the pan is warming, the heat spreads quickly to the rest of the pan.

The heat in the pan is passed on to the food. As the food gets hotter, it cooks.

The metal conducts heat away from your warm hand.

Heat spreads from the hot part of the metal to a cooler part.

See for yourself! ✋

1 See how water and chemicals in food attack metals, making them *rust* or *tarnish*. Find two glass jars and some metal objects, such as pieces of tin foil, iron nails, new copper pennies, and some old metal tableware.

Tin foil

Silver-plated spoon

Iron nails

Pennies

Stainless steel fork

2 Pour a mixture of water and vinegar into one jar until it is about 1 inch deep. Add a tablespoon of salt and some beaten raw egg, and stir in. In the other jar combine the same depth of water with a tablespoon of baking soda and a lima bean pod.

3 Put some pieces of metal into each jar, and leave them to soak for a few days. Then look closely. What effect do you think the changes in the metals will have on any food cooked in them?

Pure iron will rust

Stainless steel should stay the same.

WOW! See your face in it!

Most brand new pots and pans are shiny. This is because metals reflect light when they are polished. In fact, mirrors were made of metal until the 1500s, when they began to be made of glass. The shine soon disappears from most pans when they are used for cooking. However, stainless steel can resist the damage done by food. It is very strong, and does not rust or tarnish easily, so it keeps its shine.

Be careful not to touch hot metal handles.

29

Kitchen quiz

1 How do you have a balanced diet?

   a) By eating one type of food
   b) By eating a variety of foods
   c) By weighing your food
before eating it

2 When does your tummy rumble?

   a) When you're full
   b) When you're thirsty
   c) When you're hungry

3 What's inside a camel's hump?

   a) Fat
   b) Water
   c) Milk

4 Where are your taste buds?

   a) In your throat
   b) On your tongue
   c) In your cheeks

5 What do bacteria and mold do to food?

   a) They keep it fresh
   b) They make it go bad
   c) They make it tastier

6 What is used to make bread rise?

   a) Yeast
   b) Water
   c) Butter

7 Why do some animals swallow stones?

   a) Because there is no other food available
   b) To help grind food
   c) To clean their teeth

8 What does a gelling agent do to a liquid?

   a) It makes it bubbly
   b) It makes it rise
   c) It makes it set

9 What happens to butter at its melting point?

   a) It changes from a solid into a liquid
   b) It changes from a solid into a gas
   c) It changes from a gas into a liquid

10 What makes popcorn pop?

   a) Heating it
   b) Freezing it
   c) Soaking it

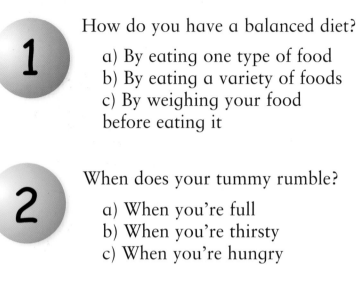

Answers on page 32

Glossary

Acids
A group of chemical substances that have a sour or sharp taste.

Alimentary canal
The long passage that stretches from the mouth to the anus.

Bacteria
Simple living things made of only one cell.

Carbohydrates
Nutrients that supply the body with energy.

Carbon dioxide
A gas found in air, and produced by the body when cells release energy from food.

Cells
The tiny living units that make up plant and animal bodies. Different types of cells do different jobs.

Colloid
A mixture containing a gelling agent and water.

Concentrated
When a large amount of a substance is mixed in with a liquid.

Conductors
Materials that, without moving, allow heat to flow through them.

Digest
To break down food into simple nutrients that the body can use.

Energy
The power needed for doing work or for action.

Enzymes
Special substances made by cells that help break down food. Used by the body during digestion.

Fats
Nutrients that are used to give energy, and to help build the body.

Fungus
A living organism (for example, a mushroom or mold), that is like a simple plant. Some fungi, like yeast, are tiny, single cells.

Gelling agent
A substance that holds on to a lot of water to form a colloid.

Glucose
A type of sugar that most cells use for energy. Glucose is carried around the body in the blood. It is also used by plants.

Grains
Hard seeds, especially from cereal plants related to grass.

Intestines
The long, thin, twisty part of the alimentary canal where food is digested and absorbed. It is divided into the small and large intestines.

Kernel
The edible center of any grain or nut that has a hard outer covering. The grain of a cereal plant.

Melting point
The temperature at which a substance turns from a solid into a liquid.

Minerals
Nutrients needed to make sure the body works correctly.

Mold
Tiny fungi that feed on the decaying remains of living things.

Nutrients
Substances found in food that are needed to keep living things alive.

Preservatives
Substances that make food stay fresh longer.

Proteins
Nutrients that are used for growth and repair.

Rust
The red-brown powder that forms on iron when it is exposed to air and water.

Senses
Parts of the nervous system (the network of cells that take messages around the body) that allows the body to keep track of what is happening.

Starch
A carbohydrate that stores energy for plants and is a useful food for animals.

Tarnish
To make a metal dull and discolored.

Taste buds
Clusters of cells inside bumps on the surface of the tongue that sense different tastes.

Vitamins
Nutrients found in small amounts in food that the body needs work correctly.

Index

Answers to the Kitchen quiz on page 30

1 b 2 c 3 a 4 b 5 b 6 a 7 b 8 c 9 a 10 a